STAFFORD CLIFF

1000
GARDEN
IDEAS

Quadrille

Plants aren't the only thing that you need to think about when you are creating a garden. In fact – with so many gardening programmes, magazine articles and books around – plants are now one of the easiest things to find, especially when there are so many plant suppliers and nurseries around the world. But what about all the other decisions you need to make? The paths, the paving, the pots, the fencing and the gate? Would you like a bench and a table, a water feature, a birdhouse or a bridge? What should they look like? How will they fit into the rest of your garden scheme? And how can you make them look more individual, more creative or more effective? Whatever you want to do, someone has done it before, and if you've ever been to visit other gardens, country houses or local garden open-days, you will have realised that this is the best way to pick up good ideas – if only you could store them away until you need them; if only you could find so many that you'd have lots of choices for every gardening problem you're ever likely to need to solve; if only you could gather them all into an album of garden ideas. now you don't need to. For the first time, they're all here – forty years of visiting gardens with a designer's eye, to spot the cleverest solutions, the best answers, the most original choices, and present them all in the most comprehensive collection of garden ideas you could ever find.

GATES

Walk up and down your street, explore your neighbourhood, your town. Why are all the front gates so boring? A front gate is an opportunity to show how individual we are, how creative, how inventive. Perhaps, because they tend to be made from either wood or metal, they perish or rust away more quickly than other garden elements like walls and paths. If your gate is at the back of the house, or in a side wall, it will be a different size and shape to one at the front. Sometimes, when we move in, they're missing altogether, and we're at a loss to know what design to choose or, indeed, if we need one at all. On the other hand, in a street where all the houses are built in the same style or the same period, maybe there is a perception that the gate belongs more to the façade of the building than to the planting or the personality of the owner. Certainly there are streets in London or Paris or Sydney or Charleston, where all the fences and gates are part of the urban architecture and you cannot change even the colour. For the rest, look around for something that suits you, your home and the way you live. Think of it as a chance to add a little design flourish that would be inappropriate on a larger scale – like a stamp on a letter.

WALLS & FENCES

The frame to your horticultural composition is the fence or wall. Start by answering three simple questions: do you want to see it or cover it up with some sort of climbing plant? Do you want to see through it or block out what is beyond? Finally, do you want to keep something out or keep something in? For various reasons, most of us need a fence, but not one so high that it blocks out the light and causes conflict with our neighbours. If you only need to define the margins of your domain, then a simple post and rail job will do. But, for most gardeners, it's one of the defining factors that finishes off the space, provides an element of protection and a vertical surface with which to be creative. And creativity is the key, because there is now an unlimited supply of possibilities, from mellow old brick, drystone or cracked pebbles, to concrete, ribbed and perforated metal, corrugated iron or glass bricks. Some are permanent; some more temporary. Some harmonise with the style of the house; others create a contrast. Some let light through; some retain the heat and block the wind. Some you can assemble yourself, buying the components and taking them home in the car; some might require a carpenter, a bricklayer or a builder; for some you might need a reclamation yard or even an antique dealer.

TILES, PATHS & PAVING

When it comes to the surface underfoot, there are a number of elements to consider, but of course it depends on the area you intend to cover. If it's a narrow front path then it will be one of the first things people see when they arrive; if it's a large area at the back of the house or in the heart of the garden, then it will contribute as much to your scheme as the planting, particularly if you look down on it from the upstairs windows. The graphic quality of what you decide to do is important both from up close as you stand on it, and from afar. But how does it 'feel' to walk on — smooth and firm, spongy and organic, or rough and uneven — or is it a combination? It could be smooth where you're meant to walk and rough where you're not. It could progress gradually from one material to another, one colour to another, or one scale to another. Do you want it to look rustic, like a path in harmony with nature, or modern and 'architectural', part of the built environment? How will it change when it's wet or even icy? When it's covered with leaves or blossom or moss? Will it turn out to be an ongoing nightmare to maintain, or will it improve with age? Lastly, think about how it sounds. Gravel will alert you to approaching visitors, but woodchip, pebbles, slate shards and glass beads all produce a variety of interesting sounds, and say a lot more about you and your flair as a creative gardener.

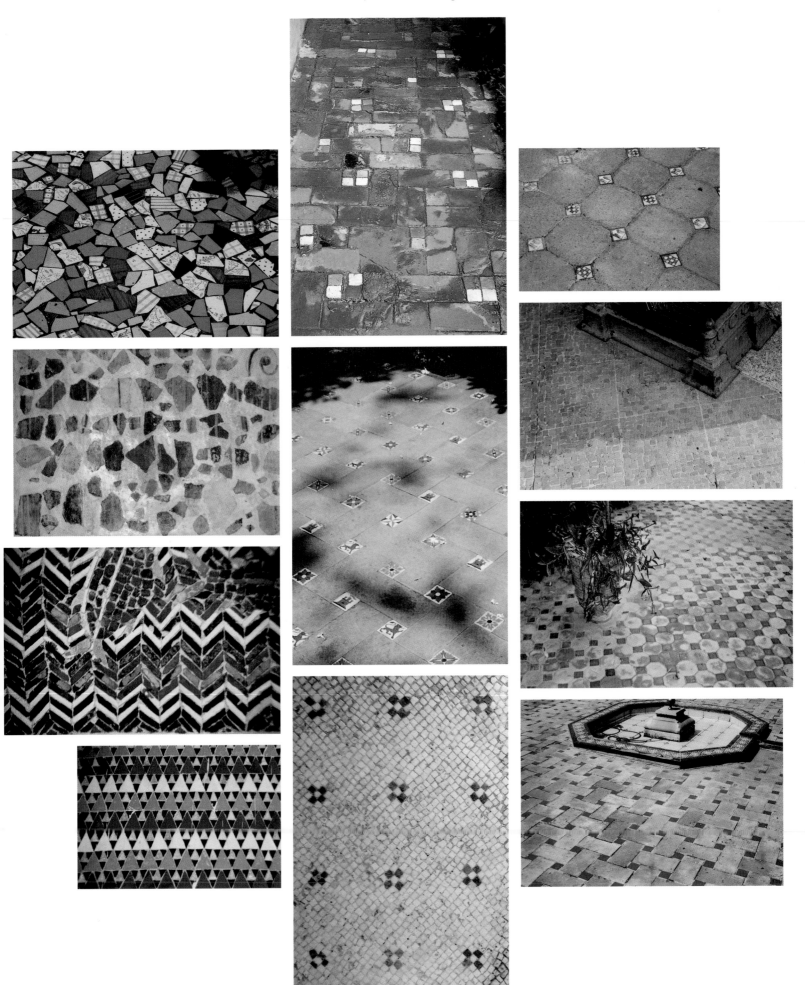

EDGING

If a garden is a poem or a short story, then edging is the punctuation and a fence is a full stop. Edgings are vital to the flow of the planting, joining one phrase to another, coordinating a number of different or similar ideas and knitting the picture together. Yet, if they are so important, why are they so often overlooked or uninspired? Look at the horizontal surfaces in a garden as a number of personalities meeting each other. Some, like flowers and low hedges, get on well together, whereas others – hard and soft characters, like lawn and path – are best kept apart. How the edging works will depend on the style of your garden; if it's rustic or cottagey your solution will be found in the countryside – rocks, little fences or, perhaps, an old log; if it's contemporary your answers are more likely to come from urban architecture and the use of modern materials – concrete, steel, slate, brick, acrylic or even glass. Finally, if you're feeling creative, consider recycling something. Blue bottles sunk upside down into the earth, broken frost-free terracotta pots, or even old dinner plates, half-embedded. Failing all else, there are the products that are made for the job: moulded tiles, glazed terracotta rope segments, latticed willow hurdles or reproduction-antique French iron railings.

STEPS

More than perhaps any other element in the garden, I think steps are the most fascinating, with the most possibilities. They take us from one level to another, they change our perspective of the space, and they present endless opportunities for creativity. From the bottom we see one aspect – the risers or upright bits; from the top we see the treads; in mid-flight we see both. So, why are they so often dull and ignored, grey concrete or drab stone? Perhaps we are afraid to do anything too creative in case it looks confusing and unsafe? Perhaps – if we have inherited them – they are too difficult to replace. Perhaps we just need inspiration. Adding different levels to a garden can be a costly and daunting prospect and, consequently, steps are usually limited to only two or three wide treads. On the other hand, many of the most fascinating gardens are hilly, with steps that wind up out of sight, turn a corner, or stop and start seemingly at will. Steps also afford all sorts of areas for planting, they need a beginning and an end, and they need edges – all providing a chance to embellish. At the same time, many homes are built on hills, or have steps – often half a dozen or so – up to the entrance. Why should they be any less important a chance for self-expression than the gate, the path or, indeed, the front door?

POTS

Pots are, perhaps, the most flexible of all the elements in the garden. You can move them around until you find the best position, you can bring them forward when the plants they contain are in flower, and you can, of course, change the plants as often as you like. You can, and I hope you will, have lots of pots in lots of shapes and sizes, like hats to top off different outfits, or bright colourful ties to dress up the same dark suit. But pots are not just for plants, they can contain water, pebbles, twigs or even fish. They are available in an abundance of different materials with a plain or matte finish, glazed in rich colours, or embellished with a multitude of designs. More elaborate containers look best with modest sculptural contents, whereas a showy cascading plant might need a simpler pot. Finally, there are the urns, the Dowager Duchesses of the pot, which have a design heritage that can be traced back to the Renaissance. Aloof on a plinth, they are an object in their own right. Though pots are currently the most fashionable design accessory in the garden don't be limited by what you see in the shops. Search out reclamation yards, specialist potteries, or even find a local potter and commission him or her to create your own shape, or copy one of the examples that follow.

CHAIRS, SEATS & BENCHES

A bench is not only a place to sit. Whether it's made from wood or concrete, stone or metal, a bench (or a seat) also functions like a piece of sculpture – an object that adds to the composition of your garden and a relief from the soft planting. The size, the form and the design of the piece – and where you place it – are as important as what it's like to sit on. It should be comfortable, but it should also look comfortable – as well as being in keeping with the size and style of your garden: classical and grand, modern and architectural, or twiggy and rustic. Some benches are meant to stay out all year round, growing more attractive as they slowly weather, acquiring a patina of moss or rust. Others are too fragile and are designed to fold away after the summer. Some of the best have tailor-made or improvised cushions that appear each morning, and some – perhaps close to the house – form part of a cluster of furniture that provides a spot for lunches or candlelit summer suppers. But, on its own, a bench is also a marker. It says that over here there is a nice viewpoint, the best vista, the most sheltered/sunny aspect or a shady, cool retreat. It signals to everyone that, if you sit for a while, you won't be disappointed.

STATUES
& OTHER OBJECTS

The tradition of having statues dotted around your garden goes back to the Italian gardens of the 16th century and beyond. They were thought to compel interest, stimulate imagination, strengthen memory and discourage trivial and selfish thoughts. The statue – particularly of the human body – had the effect of commanding your attention and perhaps, if it was a good copy of a classical work, your admiration. Nowadays, really wonderful pieces of garden statuary have become highly sought after and tend to fetch colossal prices – even those that are badly weathered and with bits missing. In fact, the more weathered the better. But such pieces can also be difficult to integrate well into a modest town garden, and mass-produced, scaled-down copies are considered as kitsch as gnomes and fairies. Consider, instead, other objects that will also give focus, create shape or add a bit of tension: old chimney pots, architectural fragments, sundials, columns, urns, obelisks – even a fallen branch or an attractively shaped rock. Alternatively, there are plenty of sculptors, potters or metalworkers making things that you might find suitable. Finally, don't forget the smaller things: think about wind chimes, mobiles and, most environmentally friendly of all, houses for birds, bats, hedgehogs and even ladybirds.

ROCKS

Rocks and stones in a garden represent millions of years of accumulated time. The Japanese used rocks as far back as the 7th century A.D. and some believed they symbolised the unchanging female, whereas plants were male. In both Japan and China, their gardens developed the art of the naturalistic landscape, with rivers, lakes and bridges. Later on, small urban courtyards used one or two large, beautifully shaped rocks to symbolise a distant mountain, and consequently they became highly prized both financially and artistically. More recently, rocks were also incorporated into aristocratic English gardens, as landscape gardeners built hillsides, waterfalls and grottos, in which a hermit was supposed to live. Today, rocks are still as important to gardens, are just as expensive and hold the same mythical qualities. It's about yin and yang. Hard and soft landscaping has been developed by garden designers to be as appropriate to a tiny town garden or a roof terrace as it is to a huge country estate. Rocks, from water-washed pebbles to jagged rocks and giant boulders, are readily available – some even pre-drilled to use as water features. But, unlike most other garden elements, it's harder to imagine the effect, plan the results, and avoid mistakes with an item that may take four men to lift.

WATER
POOLS, FOUNTAINS & BRIDGES

Every garden needs water. The plants need it to grow, birds and insects need it, and you need it, too. Water has been an intrinsic part of garden design since the Ancient Egyptians four thousand years ago. The Persians thought that no land beyond the sight of water could be considered a garden; their walled enclosures included streams and fountains that cooled the air and created what they called paradise. In Italy, during the Renaissance – utilising the hilly locations of many of the palaces – some of the most imaginative garden schemes were based on water being pumped to the top of the hill and allowing it to flow down again, passing through a multitude of ingenious spouts, jets and runnels. Grand country houses also had gardens that included natural looking ponds, lakes, rivers and streams. In your own garden the choices are more straightforward. If you don't have a spring, a well or a local river to divert, try creating your own natural looking pond, stream, canal, rill or cascade using the various techniques that are available to you today. Water can be still, its reflective surface adding extra light to your garden; it can bubble over rocks, trickle from a spout, or spray in a multitude of fountain effects. With water you will add, perhaps, the most relaxing, most magical quality of all: sound.

PERGOLAS, GAZEBOS & FOLLIES

Every country has its tradition of small garden structures. In Scandinavia, they are often intended for spending the day by the sea; in Japan, they are teahouses; in Indian palaces they were sometimes used to accommodate musicians, who would add their music to the other garden delights. In grand English gardens, miniature cottages, cabins and summerhouses were places for children to play, or adults to take tea – and there was always the possibility of the occasional illicit liaison. Some of these houses even had a fireplace and running water. At the opposite extreme were the belvederes, temples, follies and mock ruins that were often sited on distant hilltops in order to add visual interest and hint at Arcadian frivolity. More practical are the garden structures which, whilst sometimes framing a view, are primarily to support vines, roses and other climbing plants. These are the arches, the pergolas and the arbours, where the experience of walking beneath or through them, or sitting under them, is as important as their effect from afar. Whilst a long pergola is suitable only for larger spaces, or to transform an awkward area along one side of a town house garden, an arch is ideal for creating a focal point, embracing a seat or showcasing a spectacular flowering climber.

PARTERRES, HEDGES & TOPIARY

The art of pruning and trimming trees and bushes goes back to before the Romans, who practised it to excess. It was revived again in the Middle Ages and was a craze in the 17th, and again in the 19th, centuries. Hedges – whether privet, yew, box, holly, holm oak, horn beam or cypress – make an effective windbreak, a good background to plants and a way of dividing a large garden into a variety of interesting and theatrical spaces. Really big hedges can take two or three hundred years to achieve, and ingenious ladder structures to maintain. In Japan, cutting and controlling the shape of trees and shrubs is an intrinsic part of gardening, even in city squares and at traffic roundabouts. In Bangkok, and other parts of Thailand, topiary and its cousin bonsai adorn every temple and shrine. In France they developed the art of the parterre and in England we have our own take on the art, as peacocks and small dogs in village cottage gardens contrast with massive compositions of imagination and caprice on grand estates. At its most modest level, you might start with a specimen tree in the centre of the lawn, or two rosemary bushes beside the front door. Whatever you choose, they will all require the same love of living sculpture, and the same passion for pruning.

VISTAS

A vista provides a journey for the eye. It may not tell you the whole story but, like a trailer in the cinema or on TV, it gives you a view into something further away – through a gap in the hedge, under an arch of climbing roses, down a narrow pathway or through a door in a wall. The very first gardens, thousands of years ago, were walled enclosures. In the early 15th century, as Italian merchants began to build their villas outside the heat of the cities, they discovered that an opening in the wall of their garden gave them an attractive view of the countryside. Soon, the walled enclosure was removed altogether, and the view – or partial view – was the thing. Depending on where you live, the view can reveal a tower on a hilltop miles away or a pot on a stand, a piece of sculpture or a tree across the road. Vistas are about hiding and revealing, sometimes obscuring a view in order to tempt you with only a glimpse of it at first. They are the amuse bouche of gardening, the tasty morsel of which there may not be any more. Because, at its least, a vista may only be a promise of something which is not yours and which you cannot get to. But, by framing it and focussing on it, you are saying 'this is also part of my garden, and my garden, by definition, is part of the wider world'.

COLOUR

Plants are, of course, the most exciting part of gardening – the only point, some might say. Planning a garden, putting in your plants or bulbs or cuttings – and watching them grow – goes to the heart of gardening, and there can be nothing more therapeutic, more gratifying or more primal. Millions of people around the world get tremendous pleasure from visiting gardens and garden centres, looking at flowers and acquiring new varieties. In the late 19th century, the status of an English aristocrat was based, among other things, on the number of bedding plants his gardeners planted – sometimes as many as 50,000. But there is another aspect of gardening that is much more difficult to get right, and that is composition. It is the skill of a great chef to decide what goes with what to produce the most interesting flavours and bring out the best of all the ingredients. So it is with gardening, and it's not only about colour and soil and sun. Buy everything you like, stick it all in, and you'll get a hotchpotch of riotous joy. But, be more selective, restrict your colour palette, think about the size and scale of plants, the foliage colour and leaf shapes, and you will be rewarded with a much more subtle effect. Think of it as the difference between a brass band concert and a violin concerto.